Iguana
Takes a Ride

By Michele Spirn
Illustrated by Linda Howard Bittner

Scott Foresman
is an imprint of

Glenview, Illinois • Boston, Massachusetts • Chandler, Arizona •
Upper Saddle River, New Jersey

Illustrations
Linda Howard.

Photographs

Every effort has been made to secure permission and provide appropriate credit for photographic material. The publisher deeply regrets any omission and pledges to correct errors called to its attention in subsequent editions.

Unless otherwise acknowledged, all photographs are the property of Pearson Education, Inc.

16 Sergey_R/Shuttestock

ISBN 13: 978-0-328-51373-4
ISBN 10:   0-328-51373-3

11 12 13   V0FL 17 16 15

One day Iguana wanted to cross the river. It was too deep and too wide for Iguana to swim across. Iguana dipped a toe in the water. It was very cold.

"Oh, dear," he said, "I want to visit my mother. She will miss me if I can't see her. We are going to have lunch together. How will I ever cross the river?"

He looked up and down the river bank for an answer to his problem. A boatman rowed his boat toward Iguana.

The boatman said, "I will take you across the river. I will give you a safe ride. I can handle a boat well. My boat is swift and sure. It can ride the rough waves."

"How much is a ride with you?" Iguana asked.

"It will cost you only five dollars," the boatman replied.

"That is a lot of money for one boat ride," Iguana said. "I do not want to pay so much."

"No one handles a boat on the water as well as I do," said the boatman. "You should take the ride with me."

Just then Crocodile swam up to the edge of the river.

"What's happening?" he asked, and smiled, showing his sharp teeth.

"I want to cross the river to see my dear mother," Iguana said. "She is waiting to have lunch with me. The boatman wants five dollars for the ride. He says his boat is swift and sure and can handle the rough waves. Five dollars is a lot of money. I don't know if I should spend that much money."

"That *is* a lot of money," Crocodile said. "I wouldn't pay anyone so much money to take me across the river. I will take you across the river for free."

"You will?" asked Iguana happily.

"Be careful," said the boatman, who was listening. "Crocodiles are not known to be compassionate."

"What do you mean?" asked Iguana.

"They do not care about their riders like I do. You will see," said the boatman as he rowed his boat away.

"Maybe I'd better find out more before I take that ride," Iguana thought. "I will ask some others."

Iguana found a bird perched in a tree near the river.

"Bird, you fly all over and see things from high above. Should I take a ride across the river with Crocodile?" Iguana asked.

"I don't know exactly," said Bird. "I am too busy flying. I never saw anyone take a ride with Crocodile. You should ask someone else." Bird flew away.

Crocodile's mother swam up to Iguana. "Did my son tell you what a good swimmer he is? Did he mention that he has won many trophies for his good swimming? He is so mature for his age. He never plays any of those silly tricks like the other crocodiles. Plus, he's so adorable! Look at that face! He wouldn't try to trick you."

Still Iguana was not sure. He thought about what the boatman had said. Iguana kept walking. Soon he came upon a turtle.

"Turtle, do you think I should take a ride with Crocodile?" he asked.

Turtle started to answer, but then he saw Crocodile watching and pulled his head into his shell.

"I can't talk," Turtle said. "I'm resting. Come back later."

Iguana tried talking to the fish in the water. Surely they would know if a ride with Crocodile was a good idea. But when the fish saw Crocodile, they swam far, far away.

Iguana thought about everything he had heard while he lay on the branch of a tree. The bird did not know. The turtle and the fish wouldn't talk. Crocodile's mother was certainly proud of him. Was she reliable?

He thought some more. Crocodile was giving free rides. The boatman was asking for a lot of money. What should he do?

Time was passing. Iguana's mother was waiting to see him.

"If I don't go soon, I'll be too late for lunch," Iguana thought. "All the best bugs will be gone, and I'll have nothing to eat."

While Iguana thought about what he should do, a young frog hopped down to the river.

"I want to cross the river," he heard the frog say. "Who will take me?"

"I will," said the boatman.

"No, I will and for free," said Crocodile.

Iguana saw the frog talk to the boatman and the crocodile. The frog hopped back and forth. Suddenly, the frog hopped onto Crocodile's back.

Iguana watched as Crocodile swam away rapidly with the frog. Crocodile swam well and smoothly. The frog looked as if he were enjoying the ride. Iguana thought that maybe he would take the free ride with Crocodile.

Then, suddenly, about halfway across the river, Crocodile turned his head. With no warning, he ate the frog in one gulp.

When Crocodile swam back to the riverbank, Iguana was waiting for him. He made sure to stay far away from the edge of the river while he talked to Crocodile.

"Why did you eat the frog?" Iguana asked.

"I said I would give him a free ride," Crocodile said. "I never told him it would be a safe one. I never said that I wouldn't eat him."

Iguana turned and ran to the boatman. He gave the man five dollars.

"What made you take my boat instead of the free ride?" asked the boatman.

"I'd rather be safe than sorry," said Iguana.

Iguanas as Pets

Iguanas can be very good pets. They are small and easy to handle. They don't need to be walked every day like a dog, and they don't need huge cages.

They do need some special things. Iguanas and other lizards need a tank to live in. They also need lots of heat and light. They may need a place to live that's hotter than what you might like.

Iguanas also need special food. They like bugs and worms. Some people raise crickets and other bugs as well as worms at home. This way, they always have food for their iguana when they need it.